My First
Classical Music Book

By Genevieve Helsby

Illustrated by
Jason Chapman

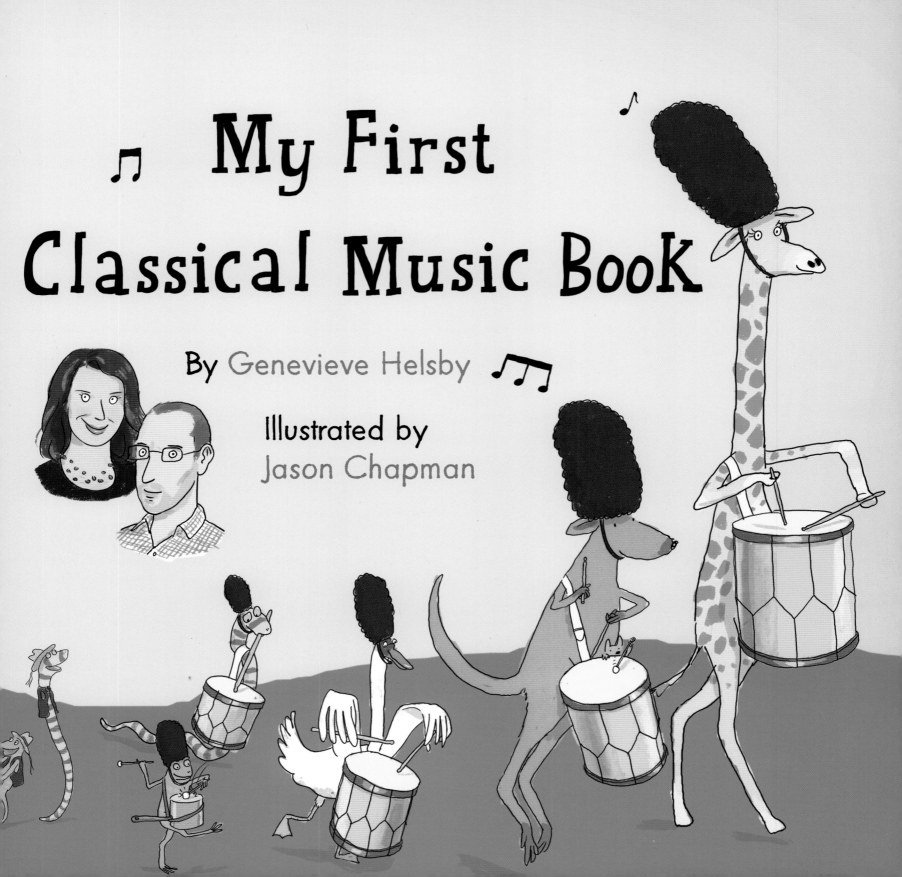

Published by Naxos Books,
an imprint of Naxos Rights International Ltd
© Naxos Books 2009

www.naxosbooks.com

Printed and bound in China by Leo Paper Group
Illustration: Jason Chapman
Design and layout: Hannah Davies, Fruition – Creative Concepts
Text editor: Genevieve Helsby
Sound editors: Malcolm Blackmoor & Sarah Butcher

ISBN: 978-1-84379-118-8

Contents

In this book, you can:

1 **READ** about classical music.
2 **LISTEN** to classical music.

Each section in the book has a 'music bird' – here he is:

He tells you about the music on the CD.

PLAY THE MUSIC

Play TRACK...
LISTEN FOR...

You will see that each piece of music has its own name, just like people do. Then we can talk about them and know which one is which.

Sometimes the music bird will tell you to listen for something. And sometimes he will ask you a question.

You can play each track as many times as you like.

Have fun!

WHEN? WHERE?

Where can you *find* music?

Music is all around us.
Music is in so many places,
we can even forget it's there!
Think about where you hear music…

On television

In the cinema

In the theatre

In a car

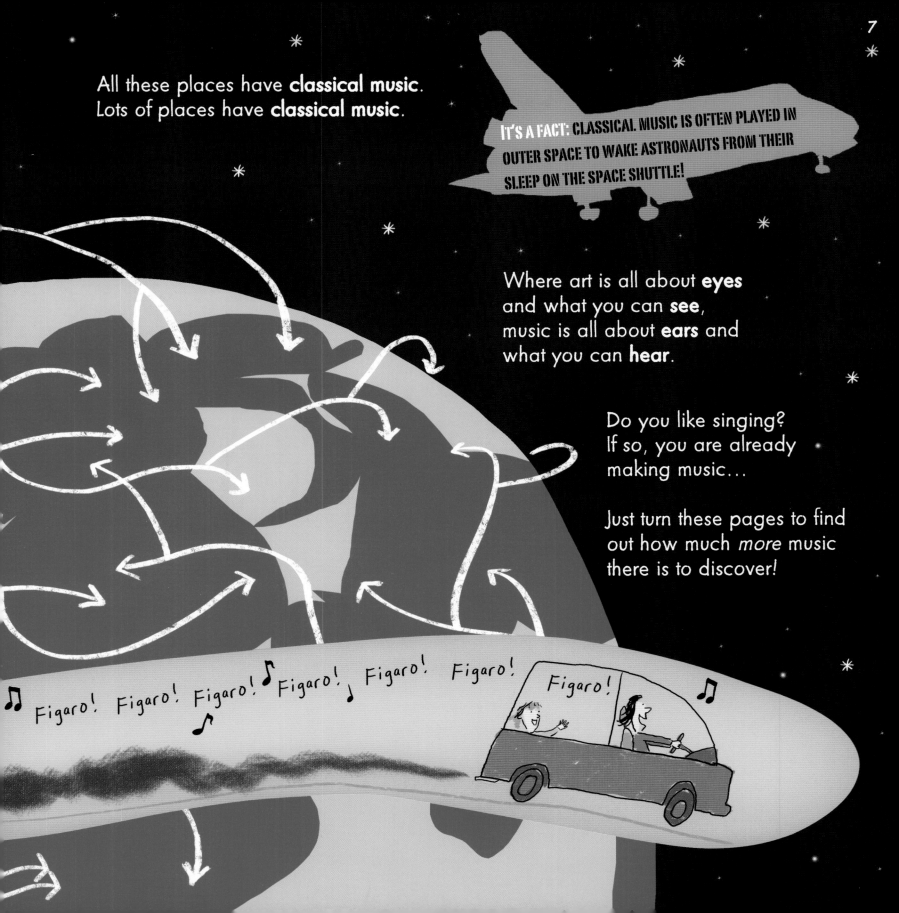

All these places have **classical music**.
Lots of places have **classical music**.

IT'S A FACT: CLASSICAL MUSIC IS OFTEN PLAYED IN OUTER SPACE TO WAKE ASTRONAUTS FROM THEIR SLEEP ON THE SPACE SHUTTLE!

Where art is all about **eyes** and what you can **see**, music is all about **ears** and what you can **hear**.

Do you like singing? If so, you are already making music...

Just turn these pages to find out how much *more* music there is to discover!

Figaro! Figaro! Figaro! Figaro! Figaro! Figaro!

Figaro!

Television & Cinema

Have you noticed that nearly *every* film and television programme has music? When you watch the screen, you use your eyes. But you also use your ears.

Television and cinema use music because it makes our imagination grow.

The Music...

Have you seen any *Harry Potter* films?
Do you know how the music goes?

Play TRACK 1
Harry Potter and the Sorcerer's Stone
('Harry's Wondrous World') by John Williams

PLAY THE MUSIC

LISTEN FOR...
High tinkles and loud crashes in the music.
These are made by **percussion** instruments.
They add to the excitement!

The man who wrote this music
is called John Williams.

When you write music for a film,
you can't just write whatever pops
into your head. You have to make
it match what people see on the screen.

So, for an exciting game of Quidditch,
John Williams writes exciting music!

Dancing

When you dance, your body is free.

Sometimes you just jiggle around.
Sometimes you do special steps.
But you always dance to **music**.

Ballet dancing is popular.
Ballet dancers can feel
balanced and beautiful.

You might dance at a party.
You don't need any lessons for that!
Some people look quite silly…
but it doesn't matter.
It's all about
having fun.

The Music...

There is a type of dance called a 'Can-Can'.
It was invented in France. You can try it when you hear the music...

PLAY THE MUSIC

Play TRACK 2
'Can-Can' from *Orpheus in the Underworld* by Offenbach

QUESTION 1
Does the music sound:
a Lively
or **b** Peaceful?
Answer on p. 64

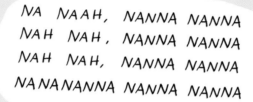

NA NAAH, NANNA NANNA
NAH NAH, NANNA NANNA
NAH NAH, NANNA NANNA
NANANANNA NANNA NANNA

This music comes from an **opera** called *Orpheus in the Underworld*.

An opera is like a big play in the theatre, but with singing instead of speaking.

To do the Can-Can:

1 Lift up your knee

2 Put it down

3 Lift it up again and stick your leg out

4 Put it down again

5 Now do the same with the other leg and keep going to the rhythm of the music

11

Concert Hall

The audience in the concert hall is excited.

Everyone is waiting for some music...

Suddenly they clap! Onto the stage walks a musician. A musician performs music.

The clapping stops. Nobody moves.

Silence.

The musician begins to play...

...and people in the audience watch and listen and smile.

The Music...

Any piece of music can be played in a concert hall.

Sometimes the music will need a lot of musicians.
But sometimes it will need only one.
It could be someone who plays the piano.

Can you imagine being that someone? There you
are – all alone – under big, bright lights. Hundreds
of faces are staring at you from the audience.
And you have to play the piano without making mistakes.

PLAY THE MUSIC

Play TRACK 3
Sonata in C major, K. 545
(Movement I. Allegro) by Mozart

LISTEN FOR...
Near the beginning, there are
lots of fast little notes that go up,
then down; up, then down.

IT'S A FACT: ONE OF THE MOST
FAMOUS AND LARGEST CONCERT
HALLS IN THE WORLD IS CARNEGIE HALL IN THE
UNITED STATES OF AMERICA. IT HAS THREE HALLS
AND SEATS OVER 2,800 PEOPLE!

Weddings

What does a wedding make you think of?

A cake?

A church?

A big party?

A wedding *can* have all these things.

But even if the wedding is in a hot air balloon, there is usually some music, somewhere...

And after the bit when the couple is married, the *party* begins! And a party needs music, too.

JUST MARRIED

The Music...

Joseph Haydn wrote great music.
He was short and not very handsome.
But he was a nice man with a good sense of humour.

He is sometimes called the 'father of the string quartet'.
It basically means that he invented this kind of music.

A **string quartet** is music for four instruments: two violins, one viola and one cello. (Find out more about these instruments on pages 38 & 39.)

You often find string quartets at weddings!

PLAY THE MUSIC

Play TRACK 4
String Quartet, Op. 33
No. 5 (Movement III.
Scherzo) by Haydn

QUESTION 2
Would you describe
this piece as:
a Still
or **b** Jerky?
Answer on p. 64

IT'S A FACT: ONE OF THE MOST-PLAYED WEDDING MARCHES IS BY FELIX MENDELSSOHN. HE WROTE IT IN 1842 FOR SHAKESPEARE'S PLAY 'A MIDSUMMER NIGHT'S DREAM'.

A **composer** writes music. Haydn and Mendelssohn were composers.

Theatre

Music and the theatre are good friends. Musicals and operas are both performed in a theatre – and they're *full* of music. Even ordinary plays often have music.

But today we have DVDs and cinema – so why do we want the theatre?

Because the theatre is *real*...

...and anything could happen!

An actor could even forget what to say, or trip over. But if this happens, the show must keep going!

Musicals and operas are both like plays but with music instead of speech.

DOINK

The Music...

Peer Gynt is a play. When it was written 150 years ago, a man called Grieg composed music to go with it. These days, the music is more famous than the play!

At one point in the play, Peer Gynt sneaks into the castle of the Mountain King.

But the King's trolls spot him!

The trolls and the King chase Peer Gynt...
...and *finally*, he manages to escape.

PLAY THE MUSIC

Play TRACK 5
Peer Gynt Suite No. 1 ('In the Hall of the Mountain King') by Grieg

LISTEN FOR...
• Peer Gynt's quiet footsteps at the beginning as he enters the castle
• The music getting faster...

PEOPLE

The people in *this* book are called **composers**.

A composer is a person who makes up music and then writes it down.

An author writes a story.
A composer writes a piece of music.

Tum Tum Tumpty Tum

No

Tum Tum Tumpty Tum Tiddly Pom

nearly

Tum Tum Tumpty TUUUUM

Perfect!

No

Tum Tum Tiddle Tum

How should I start?

A composer's head is *full* of musical ideas.
Sometimes it's hard to sort them out.

There have been thousands of composers.
But only some of them are famous.

George Frideric
Handel

(born in 1685 • died in 1759)

Do you think a year is a long time?
What about two years?
What about **300** years?

The composer called Handel lived so long
ago that he wore a wig and nobody
laughed at him. 300 years ago, it was
normal for a man to wear a wig.

This Handel has nothing to do with a *door*
handle. His name is a German name: he was
a German composer who moved to England.

The Music...

In 1749 the King of England, George II, asked Mr Handel for some music to be played at his big fireworks display.

So Handel, wearing his wig, wrote *Music for the Royal Fireworks*. It was grand music for a grand occasion.

Thousands of people came to Green Park, London to watch. The fireworks sizzled and popped while 100 musicians played Handel's music.

The music was so brilliant, people thought it was better than the fireworks!

What do *you* think?

1749

Dear Mr. Handel

I'm having a party with lots of fireworks and wondered if you could come along and give us some music?

Best wishes
George II (King)

PLAY THE MUSIC

Play TRACK 6
Music for the Royal Fireworks
('La Réjouissance')
by Handel

LISTEN FOR...
The bright and energetic tune, played by trumpets

The fireworks are good but the music is brilliant!

We agree.

Johann Sebastian Bach

(born in 1685 • died in 1750)

Here is a picture of Johann Sebastian Bach:

Yes, Bach wore a wig just like Handel did!
Handel and Bach were alive during the same time,
when lots of men wore them.

Bach was a German composer.
And he played the **organ**.

The organ is the biggest musical instrument of all.
It has a keyboard, like the piano.

Bach had twenty children!
And he still had time to write magnificent music.

You pronounce 'Bach' a bit
like 'bark' – as in the bark of
a dog or the bark of a tree.

The Music...

Bach sometimes played his own music on the organ.

The organ is like a friendly musical monster. It has pipes, pedals, keys and other buttons to press. It can be **VERY LOUD**! But it can be quiet and wonderful too.

Bach wrote a famous piece for the organ called Toccata and Fugue in D minor.

Listen to how powerful it sounds at the beginning!

PLAY THE MUSIC

Play TRACK 7
Toccata and Fugue in D minor by J.S. Bach

QUESTION 3
Does the music go on and on or does it have little gaps where you hear no sound?
Answer on p. 64

Wolfgang Amadeus Mozart

(born in 1756 • died in 1791)

Mozart is SO famous, you can even find his head on the top of chocolates.

His head was a special head. It was full of music, even when he was a small boy. This music was just bursting to get out!

At five years old, little Wolfgang started to compose his own pieces. And he could play the piano and violin.

Mozart liked to have fun. Even when he was a grown-up, he could be cheeky and playful. And his music is fun, too! It is full of energy.

He only lived to the age of 35, but his name shines like a star.

We often use a composer's last name only. So 'Wolfgang Amadeus Mozart' is just 'Mozart'.

The Music...

An **opera** is like a play, except the people on stage *sing* to each other. Mozart was really good at writing operas. *The Magic Flute* is one of his best.

In *The Magic Flute*, Papageno is the bird-catcher. He is dressed up like a big colourful bird (so that the real birds don't spot him).

Play TRACK 8
'Papageno's Song'
from *The Magic Flute*
by Mozart

LISTEN FOR...
Papageno's pan pipes!
He plays five quick little notes,
up high – twice in a row.
You can hear them first at 0:21.

PLAY THE MUSIC

Pan pipes are little pipes joined together to look a bit like a fan.

On track 8, Papageno is playing his pan pipes. And he sings 'I am a bird-catcher!'

The words are in German.

Listen to his pretty tune – or 'melody'. And can you hear his little pan pipes?

Ludwig van Beethoven

(born in 1770 • died in 1827)

It's very hard to find a picture of Beethoven smiling.
Actually, he looks quite grumpy.
He *was* quite grumpy.
But he was good at writing music.

The big thing Beethoven did was to have *new ideas*.

He was bold and daring. Music like his had never been heard before.

Poor Beethoven even went deaf... but he still composed music!
He could hear in his head the sounds he wanted and he wrote them down.

The Music...

Beethoven liked going for walks. He liked nature: the trees, the birds, the weather.

So he decided to write some music all about nature. It is called his 'Pastoral' Symphony.

Part of this symphony is called 'Thunderstorm'. When you listen to track 9, imagine that you are asleep in bed… all is calm… and then suddenly there is a rumble of thunder! And again!!!!! CRASH!!!!!

PLAY THE MUSIC

Play TRACK 9
Symphony No. 6 'Pastoral' (IV. 'Thunderstorm') by Beethoven

QUESTION 4
The thunderstorm begins at 0:27. Before this, is the music:
a Quiet
or **b** Noisy?
Answer on p. 64

A **symphony** is a long piece of music for an orchestra (a big group of instruments).

Johannes
Brahms

(born in 1833 • died in 1897)

Johannes Brahms looks a bit like Father Christmas…
but without a red coat. And he didn't say 'ho ho ho'.

But he was a large man, with a long beard.
And he collected toy soldiers!

Brahms's music is quite *serious*.
But this doesn't mean it is boring.

Brahms sometimes thought he wasn't
good enough to follow Beethoven,
the big musical hero.

But he didn't need to worry!
He became
a hero too.

The Music...

Some composers want their music to tell a story.
But Brahms decided that music and stories were separate things.

He wrote just music – on its own. It wasn't supposed to make you think of fairies or thunder or birds... it was simply *music* – full stop.

Does that sound dull? Well, as you can hear, it isn't!
Listen to one of his lively Hungarian Dances...

PLAY THE MUSIC

Play TRACK 10
Hungarian Dance No. 5 by Brahms

LISTEN FOR...
Three quick crashing sounds
at 0:27 and then again at 0:30.
These are made by cymbals – metal dishes.

Pyotr Il'yich Tchaikovsky

(born in 1840 • died in 1893)

Tchaikovsky was a Russian composer full of *feelings*.
He felt sad more than he felt happy. Poor Tchaikovsky.

But sometimes he didn't laugh *or* cry.
Instead, he took his pen and paper and wrote music.
All his feelings poured into his music.

This music can make *other* people
laugh or cry when they hear it.
And people love listening to it,
even when they cry!

The Music...

Tchaikovsky wrote a lot of **ballet** music.
Ballets are full of music and dancing.

His ballet called *The Nutcracker* is about a little girl called Clara.
She dreams that she and her imaginary prince
travel to a magical land full of sweets!

The people in this Land of Sweets are dancing,
including the Sugar Plum Fairy...

PLAY THE MUSIC

Play TRACK 11
'Dance of the Sugar Plum Fairy'
from *The Nutcracker* by Tchaikovsky

LISTEN FOR...
A tinkly sound! This is an instrument
called a celeste and it is playing the tune.
Imagine the Sugar Plum Fairy twirling around...

Igor Stravinsky

(born in 1882 • died in 1971)

When we think of Igor Stravinsky, we think of **rhythm**.

Rhythm in music is what makes you tap your feet.
Rhythm in music is what makes you nod your head and smile.
Rhythm in music is what makes you get up and dance.

Stravinsky *played* with rhythm. He created extraordinary sounds.
And he helped classical music in the 20th century to enter
a new and exciting time.

We can think of Stravinsky's rhythms like colourful
patterns in music. The patterns are spiky and jerky and
interesting, but all the shapes fit perfectly together like a jigsaw.

This music is *clever* music!

The Music...

When Stravinsky came along, ballet got really exciting!
His ballet music is full of funny rhythms.

He wrote a ballet about a puppet called Petrushka.
When the ballet begins, poor Petrushka is all floppy.
But then he comes to life – on his own!
He can *feel* things, even though he is a puppet.

With two other puppets, Petrushka leaps up and dances!

Play TRACK 12
'Russian Dance' from *Petrushka* by Stravinsky

QUESTION 5
This piece begins quite fast. Does the speed
stay the same until the end or does it
change in the middle?
Answer on p. 64

John Adams

(born in 1947 • still alive!)

John Adams is the odd one out in our book.
Why?
Because he's still alive!

He is an American composer who has written 'minimalist' music.
Minimalist music is based on simple ideas.
The ideas change a bit each time you hear them.

A lot of people like this kind of music. Listening to it is like staring at a
fire, or at the sea: you find yourself stuck there, just watching, listening…

The Music...

John Adams chooses fun titles for his pieces.
One of them is called *Short Ride in a Fast Machine*.

When you listen to it, imagine you are in a fast machine: a racing car, perhaps.
Fasten your seatbelt!

PLAY THE MUSIC

Play TRACK 13
Short Ride in a Fast Machine
   by Adams

QUESTION 6
Which is stronger in this piece:
a Melody (a tune)
or **b** Rhythm?
Answer on p. 64

INSTRUMENTS

What is an instrument?

In music, an instrument is what you use to make sound. The main instruments in classical music are grouped into families.

Some instruments have strings to make their sound.
Meet the **String family**…

You will find the String family on pages 38–41.
It is quite a close family.
The Strings don't argue.

Some instruments, made of wood or metal, have a hole for blowing down.
Meet the **Woodwind family**…

You will find the Woodwind family on pages 42–46.
They are quite different, but they all like playing solos.

Some instruments are made of brass.
Meet the **Brass family**…

The Brass family is next door to
the Woodwind family, on pages 47–49.
They are all loud in this family,
especially the Trumpets.

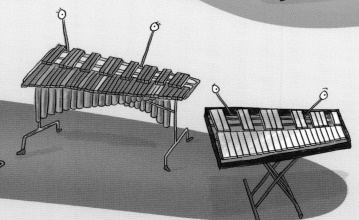

Some instruments are shaken or tapped
or struck (hit carefully!) to make a sound.
Meet the **Percussion family**…

You will find the Percussion family on pages
50–53. It's a huge family, of all ages.
And they were born in many
different countries.

Some instruments have keyboards.
Meet the **Keyboard family**…

You will find the Keyboard family on pages
54–55. Everyone in this family is tall or fat.
But there aren't many of them.

A few of these instruments
have come to say hello.
Let's meet them…

Violin

The violin is a bit like a human body: it has a 'neck', a 'back', a 'belly', and it can sing!

But to make it sing, you have to play it. You can:

1 Pull or push the bow across the violin's strings.
2 Pluck the strings with your fingers.

In the string family, the violin is a show-off. It can sound fantastic.

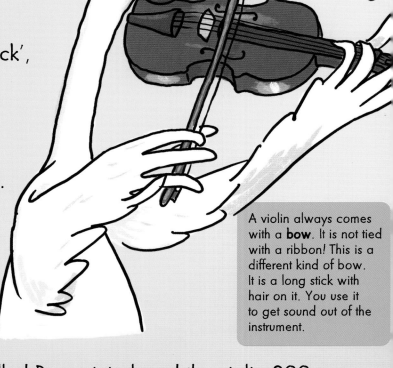

A violin always comes with a **bow**. It is not tied with a ribbon! This is a different kind of bow. It is a long stick with hair on it. You use it to get sound out of the instrument.

The Music...

A man called Paganini played the violin 200 years ago. He was so good, people called him a wizard. His fingers danced, like little acrobats, all over the violin. He *wrote* music, too...

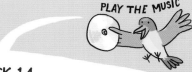

PLAY THE MUSIC

A viola is a bigger violin.

Play TRACK 14
Violin Caprice No. 16 by Paganini

LISTEN FOR...
The violin sounds high and then it sounds low – the music goes up and down, up and down – a bit like a helter skelter!

Cello

The cello is a very big violin.

Because it is so big, you don't stand up when you play it. You sit down and put it on the floor between your legs.

It has a spike on its bottom! This is like having grips on your trainers: it makes sure the cello doesn't slide across the floor.

The cello is a beautiful instrument.

The Music...

PLAY THE MUSIC

Play TRACK 15
'The Swan' from *The Carnival of the Animals* by Saint-Saëns

LISTEN FOR...
This piece is called 'The Swan'.
- Imagine a white swan, gliding across the water.
- The rippling water in the background is played by the piano.

QUESTION 7
Would you describe this music as: **a** Lively, **b** Bouncy or **c** Smooth?
Answer on p. 64

The Carnival of the Animals was written by the composer Saint-Saëns. In this piece, instruments sound like animals. The cello sounds like a swan, and the double bass (on the next page!) sounds like an elephant.

Double Bass

The double bass is HUGE!

It's a bit like trying to play a wardrobe…
except that *this* wardrobe is curvy and it has strings.

Pitch
Pitch is about how low or high a sound is.

In animals:
The tweet of a little bird is a high sound.
The roar of a big bear is a low sound.

And in music:
A little instrument makes a high sound.
A big instrument makes a low sound.

So the double bass, being HUGE,
makes a *really* low sound.

The Music...

PLAY THE MUSIC

Play TRACK 16
'The Elephant' from *The Carnival
of the Animals* by Saint-Saëns

LISTEN FOR...
This piece is called 'The Elephant'.
Imagine an elephant, bumbling along, its
trunk swinging gently to and fro… The very
beginning is played by the piano. Then the
double bass joins in.

QUESTION 8
Does this music seem:
a Slow and heavy
or **b** Fast and light?
Answer on p. 64

Guitar

Many people love the guitar.

In pop music, the guitar is usually electric.
It has an amplifier, and it can sound very loud!

In classical music, the guitar is called an 'acoustic' guitar.
It doesn't have any leads or plugs or extra bits. It is simple.

You pluck or strum the strings of a guitar with your fingers –
there is no bow to pull across the strings.

The Music...

The guitar is popular in Spain. Listen to the
'Spanish Dance' on the CD, played by just one
guitar. It's quite sad and moody for a dance.

PLAY THE MUSIC

Play TRACK 17
Danze española No. 5
'Andaluza' by Granados

QUESTION 9
Is the guitarist:
a Bowing the strings
b Plucking the strings
or **c** Blowing through the guitar?
Answer on p. 64

Recorder

A recorder is a tube with holes in.
You blow down the tube, and out comes a sound.

Simple!

You cover different holes with your fingers for
different notes. The recorder is the easiest
woodwind instrument to play.

The Music...

The recorder was especially important in classical music 300 years ago.
And 300 years ago, there was a German composer who liked the recorder a lot.
His name was Telemann.

Telemann was famous, popular and talented.
Talented Telemann wrote so much music that he's in
The Guinness Book of Records!

PLAY THE MUSIC

Ich bin ein Rekordbrecher!
(I'm a record-breaker!)

Play TRACK 18
Recorder Suite in A minor
('Les Plaisirs') by Telemann

QUESTION 10
Does the recorder sound as if it
is: **a** Running, or **b** Walking?
Answer on p. 64

Flute

Have you ever blown across the top of a bottle and made a sound? It's not easy. But when you get it right, a clear note comes out. This is how you play the flute.

It is a tube of shiny metal with holes and keys. You hold it out to the side when you play.

The flute can be full of energy. It is good at music that flutters around like a little bird. But it can make a soft and gentle sound too.

PLAY THE MUSIC

The Music...

The last time we met Mozart, he was busy with a *magic* flute. This time, he is busy with a normal one.

In this piece, he asks the flute to play with the harp. Listen and see if you think they sound good together!

Hi!

Hello!

Play TRACK 19
Flute and Harp Concerto
(Movement I. Allegro) by Mozart

LISTEN FOR...
A conversation! But not a conversation between two people. It is between the flute and the harp. The flute starts. Then the harp answers the flute. Then they both play together. Then it is the flute... the harp answers... and so on.

QUESTION 11
Are there other instruments in this piece or just the flute and harp?
Answer on p. 64

A **harp** is a very large instrument with strings. The strings are plucked.

Clarinet

The clarinet is another tube to blow down. But this one is decorated like a Christmas tree, with silver keys. It has a very thin piece of wood on the mouthpiece. This is the reed.

In a piece called *Peter and the Wolf*, the clarinet is the cat! A clarinet's sound *is* like a cat. It can…

…creep along…

…leap up high…

…crouch down low…

…scamper around…

And it is smooth and velvety.

Oboe

An oboe looks a bit like a clarinet. But it's smaller and makes a thinner, sharper sound. In *Peter and the Wolf*, it plays the duck!

Grrr

Quack

Bassoon

A bassoon is a big, brown woodwind instrument. It makes a low sound. In *Peter and the Wolf*, it plays the grumbling grandfather!

The Music...

In *Peter and the Wolf*, a boy called Peter plays in the meadow. There is a cat in the meadow. The cat is played by the clarinet. This is what happens:

LOOK OUT!

Peter and the Wolf was written by a Russian composer called Sergey Prokofiev.

YUM YUM

TUM TEE TUM

1 The cat is creeping quietly behind a bird…
'Yum yum,' thinks the cat,
'I'll get my paws on that…'
listen for the clarinet

PLAY THE MUSIC

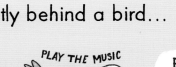

2 Peter shouts to warn the bird!
listen for a sudden crash and bouncy strings at 0:48

Play TRACK 20
'The Cat' from *Peter and the Wolf* by Prokofiev

QUESTION 12
Which instrument sounds higher:
a Clarinet, or **b** Flute?
Answer on p. 64

3 The bird flies up into the tree.
listen for the flute at 0:53

4 The duck quacks at the cat.
listen for the oboe at 1:00 and 1:06

5 The cat crawls around the tree that the bird is in, thinking 'what shall I do now?'
listen for the clarinet at 1:16; then the clarinet and flute at 1:33

See if you can hear these things in the music!

Later in the piece, a wicked wolf appears and swallows the duck! But clever Peter traps the wolf and hunters take him away to the zoo. As they go, you can still hear the poor little duck quacking inside the wolf's stomach.

Saxophone

The saxophone likes to be free.

It's relaxed and cool.
And its favourite music is jazz music.

It's really good at messing around,
making strange noises. It can
even growl and laugh!

The Music...

Sometimes, the saxophone has little solos
in the orchestra. Here, it has a BIG solo
– all the way through. The music is for
saxophone and string instruments.
So the saxophone is in the spotlight.

Play TRACK 21
Concerto for alto saxophone
and strings by Glazunov

QUESTION 13
Between 1:02 and 1:25,
would you describe the
saxophone's music as:
a Jumpy
or **b** Smooth?
Answer on p. 64

Alto

Bass

Tenor

There are different
sizes of saxophone
– from a tiddly
little one to a big
chunky one.

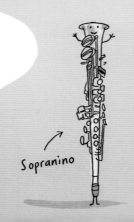

Sopranino

Trumpet

It's difficult to hide a trumpet.

It is bold.
It is bossy.
It is loud.

When you play a brass instrument, you don't put your lips round the mouthpiece like a lollipop. You press your lips *onto* the mouthpiece, and then blow!

The trumpet is an important member of the orchestra.
It is made of brass.

The trumpet has valves.
You press these down to help you play different notes.

Play TRACK 22
'Triumphal March' from *Aida* by Verdi

LISTEN FOR...
Bright, bold trumpets playing a bright, happy, victorious tune!

The Music...

Aida is an opera. It has an Egyptian princess, a brave captain, true love and fierce battles.

When the captain returns from a battle, there is a march to celebrate his victory. And a strong, bold captain deserves strong, bold trumpets!

When Mozart was a little boy, he was scared of the trumpet!

Trombone

The trombone is famous for its slide.
The slide is a tube in a long 'U'
shape. Your right arm pulls
it out and pushes it in.

Why?

The slide makes different notes sound.
A trumpet has valves but a trombone
has a slide instead.

There are other reasons
to play the trombone, too:
It is a grand instrument.
It makes a grand sound.
You *look* grand when you play it.

French Horn

This looks like a solid brass
lump of spaghetti.
It has a smooth sound.

Tuba

This is so big that you
hug it when you play.
Its sound is large and low.

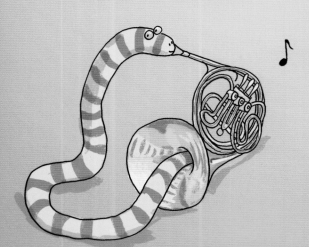

The Music...

Often, trombones team up in the orchestra.
When they play together, the sound is loud and powerful.

One German composer *loved* a loud noise!
His name was Richard Wagner.

He thought trombones were great.
And the more trombones there were, the happier he was.

PLAY THE MUSIC

Play **TRACK 23**
Overture to *Tannhäuser*
by Wagner

LISTEN FOR...
The trombones! They
play the strong tune.

Drums

There are many kinds of drum.

TSSHHH

Snare

Bongos

Tom-toms

Bass

BANG

BANG

Each drum makes a different kind of sound.
To play them, you strike them with beaters or sticks. Easy!
Well… it *is* easy to make a sound.
But it isn't so easy to make the *right* sound in the *right* place.

If you're playing the drums in an orchestra, you have to read the music carefully so that you know exactly when to go 'bang'.
Otherwise, it's easy to go 'bang' when you shouldn't and spoil everything!

Each drum has a 'skin' stretched across the top. Sometimes it is animal skin, but sometimes it is plastic. You strike the skin with a beater.

OOPS!

BANG

The Music...

A snare drum makes a kind of dry, rattling sound.
It's good for attracting attention!

Here it is in a march. See if you can march
like a soldier in time to the music!

PLAY THE MUSIC

Play TRACK 24
Semper Fidelis march
by Sousa

LISTEN FOR...
The snare drums
at the beginning.

QUESTION 14
When all the instruments
come in at 0:42 and the
music gets louder, are the
snare drums still playing?
Answer on p. 64

Xylophone & Glockenspiel

The xylophone and the glockenspiel both have bars.
These make different notes when you strike
them with beaters.

The shorter bars make a higher sound.
The longer bars make a lower sound.

The xylophone is big
with wooden bars.
It makes a dry,
wooden sound.

The glockenspiel is
small with metal bars.
It makes a happy,
tinkling sound.

The Music...

Do you know what a fossil is? It is the dry remains of something that lived thousands – or millions – or *billions* of years ago! Fossils come in all shapes and sizes. They are like interesting rocks.

In *The Carnival of the Animals*, there is a section for fossils. The dry sound of the xylophone is perfect for these!

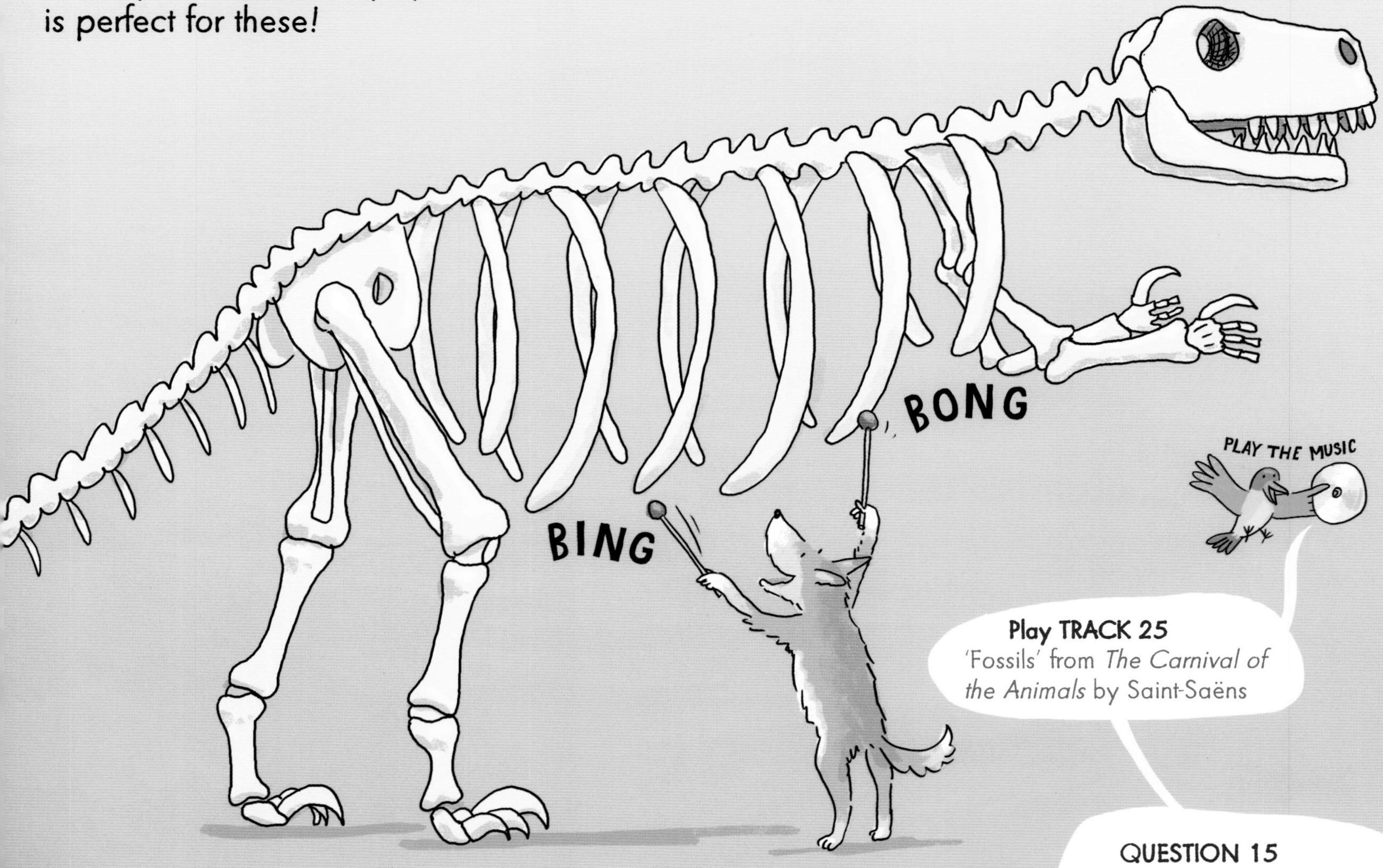

BONG

BING

PLAY THE MUSIC

Play TRACK 25
'Fossils' from *The Carnival of the Animals* by Saint-Saëns

QUESTION 15
At 0:17, the xylophone stops. Does it come back?
Answer on p. 64

Piano

The piano is all about hands and fingers.

There are 88 keys for your fingers to press: 52 white ones and 36 black ones.
If you press one key, you hear one note. If you press two keys, you hear two notes.

If you pressed 88 keys, you would hear 88 notes.
But you are not an octopus with fingers,
so you can't press 88 keys together.

And if you *did* press 88 keys,
it would sound like a big,
fat NOISE for no reason.

When composers write music,
they choose the keys for you:
their music tells you which ones to press.

But the special thing
about the piano is that
you *can* play many
notes at once. And
you can play them
quietly... or LOUDLY!

The Music...

Sergei Rachmaninov was a Russian composer with enormous hands.

These hands could stretch out and play together notes which are far apart on the piano.

Rachmaninov wrote music to fit his giant hands. It is hard to play but it always sounds full of life!

A 'pianist' is somebody who plays the piano.

PLAY THE MUSIC

Play TRACK 26
Polka italienne by Rachmaninov

LISTEN FOR...
The music is a polka – a polka is a dance. It is *rhythmic*: you can feel the beat of it, you could dance to it, it is lively.

QUESTION 16
There are two sections to the piece. The first is in a *minor* key (serious, mysterious). At 0:16, the music changes to a *major* key (playful, happy). Does the music end in a:
a Minor key
or **b** Major key?
Answer on p. 64

The Orchestra

An orchestra is a team of musicians. The musicians play different instruments.
So there are lots of sounds.

The team is very organised. It is controlled by the **conductor**,
who stands in front of all the players. The conductor waves
his arms a lot and makes faces. It's like a special language
which only the musicians can understand.

Orchestras can be big or small.
A normal 'symphony orchestra'
has about 100 people.

Sometimes the conductor holds a little stick called a baton.
All the musicians have to watch that little baton.
It makes sure they don't play
too slowly or too fast.

BANG

The Music...

We know a lot about the planet earth. We live on it!
But there are other planets too. They sit in the sky, millions of miles
away. Nearly 100 years ago, an English composer called Gustav
Holst thought:

'These planets are *so* exciting!
I'm going to write music about them!'

So Holst wrote *The Planets*. It is for a
big orchestra and has seven sections:
Mars, Venus, Mercury, Jupiter, Saturn, Uranus, Neptune.

Let's listen to Mars. Mars is a planet named after the
god of *war*. So it's an angry planet for an angry god.

PLAY THE MUSIC

Play TRACK 27
'Mars, the Bringer of
War' from *The Planets*
by Holst

LISTEN FOR...
The music starts very quietly
then gets louder... and louder...
with more brass instruments.
Mars is getting angry!

If you look really carefully and you're
very lucky, you can see Mars in the
sky at night: it glows red.

Voice

The voice is the oldest instrument in the world.
You don't need anything except your own body!
People all over the world sing.

They do it in the bath.
They do it in the car.
They do it in the kitchen, just singing to 'lah'.

But to be a really good singer, you need to train properly.
The voice is part of your body but you still have to learn how to use it well.

We call a group of singers a **choir**.

The Music...

Do you remember the man with the fireworks who wore a wig? He's back! This time Mr Handel has written a piece for a choir and an orchestra.

The piece is about the life of Jesus Christ. It is called *Messiah*. Quite soon in *Messiah*, the choir sings 'For unto us a child is born'.

The child is Jesus, and they are celebrating his birth.

Play TRACK 28
'For unto us a child is born' from *Messiah* by Handel

QUESTION 17

There is one word from the title that the singers seem to get stuck on — they sing a lot of fast notes on this word. Which word is it?

Answer on p. 64

That is the end of

My First
Classical Music Book

BUT... there is a lot more
classical music to discover!

Once you know which pieces you
like best on the CD, you can try
to find more like them.

Try exploring **www.naxos.com**.

And if you're not already learning
an instrument, perhaps now
is the time to begin!

Enjoy your musical journey!

The Music

Full Details of All Tracks on the CD

[1] **Williams:** *Harry Potter and the Sorcerer's Stone*
('Harry's Wondrous World')
Royal Liverpool Philharmonic Orchestra; Carl Davis

1:35
8.570505

[2] **Offenbach:** 'Can-Can' from *Orpheus in the Underworld*
Slovak State Philharmonic Orchestra; Johannes Wildner

2:15
8.550924

[3] **Mozart:** Sonata in C major, K. 545 (Movement I. Allegro)
Jenő Jandó, piano

3:04
8.550446

[4] **Haydn:** String Quartet, Op. 33 No. 5 (Movement III. Scherzo)
Kodály Quartet

1:44
8.550788

[5] **Grieg:** *Peer Gynt* Suite No. 1 ('In the Hall of the Mountain King')
Norrköping Symphony Orchestra; Mats Rondin

2:18
8.557426

[6] **Handel:** *Music for the Royal Fireworks* ('La Réjouissance')
Aradia Ensemble; Kevin Mallon

3:09
8.557764

7   **J.S. Bach:** Toccata and Fugue in D minor, BWV 565   3:05
Wolfgang Rübsam, organ   8.553859

8   **Mozart:** 'Papageno's Song' from *The Magic Flute*   2:52
Georg Tichy, Papageno; Budapest Failoni Chamber Orchestra;
Michael Halász   8.660030–31

9   **Beethoven:** Symphony No. 6 (IV. 'Thunderstorm')   2:54
Nicolaus Esterházy Sinfonia; Béla Drahos   8.553474

10   **Brahms:** *Hungarian Dance* No. 5 (orch. Schmeling)   2:15
Budapest Symphony Orchestra; István Bogár   8.550110

11   **Tchaikovsky:** 'Dance of the Sugar Plum Fairy' from *The Nutcracker*   2:12
Slovak Radio Symphony Orchestra; Ondrej Lenárd   8.550515

12   **Stravinsky:** 'Russian Dance' from *Petrushka*   2:36
Philharmonia Orchestra; Robert Craft   8.557500

13   **Adams:** *Short Ride in a Fast Machine*   2:45
Bournemouth Symphony Orchestra; Marin Alsop   8.559031

14   **Paganini:** Violin Caprice No. 16   1:33
Ilya Kaler, violin   8.550717

15   **Saint-Saëns:** 'The Swan' from *The Carnival of the Animals*   3:06
Slovak Radio Symphony Orchestra; Ondrej Lenárd   8.550335

16   **Saint-Saëns:** 'The Elephant' from *The Carnival of the Animals*   1:36
Slovak Radio Symphony Orchestra; Ondrej Lenárd   8.550335

17   **Granados:** *Danze española* No. 5 'Andaluza'   2:02
Norbert Kraft, guitar   8.553999

[18] **Telemann:** Recorder Suite in A minor ('Les Plaisirs') — 1:56
Daniel Rothert, recorder; Cologne Chamber Orchestra; Helmut Müller-Brühl — 8.554018

[19] **Mozart:** Flute and Harp Concerto (Movement I. Allegro) — 2:20
Patrick Gallois, flute; Fabrice Pierre, harp — 8.557011

[20] **Prokofiev:** 'The Cat' from *Peter and the Wolf* — 1:43
Slovak Radio Symphony Orchestra; Ondrej Lenárd — 8.550335

[21] **Glazunov:** Concerto for alto saxophone and strings — 1:44
Theodore Kerkezos, saxophone; Philharmonia Orchestra; Martyn Brabbins — 8.557063

[22] **Verdi:** 'Triumphal March' from *Aida* — 1:35
Slovak Radio Symphony Orchestra; Oliver Dohnányi — 8.553167

[23] **Wagner:** Overture to *Tannhäuser* — 1:00
Slovak Radio Symphony Orchestra; Michael Halász — 8.556657

[24] **Sousa:** *Semper Fidelis* — 1:37
Keith Brion; Royal Artillery Band — 8.559092

[25] **Saint-Saëns:** 'Fossils' from *The Carnival of the Animals* — 1:18
Slovak Radio Symphony Orchestra; Ondrej Lenárd — 8.550335

[26] **Rachmaninov:** *Polka italienne* — 1:35
Balász Szokolay, piano — 8.550107

[27] **Holst:** 'Mars, the Bringer of War' from *The Planets* — 2:11
Royal Scottish National Orchestra; David Lloyd-Jones — 8.555776

[28] **Handel:** 'For unto us a child is born' from *Messiah* — 2:23
The Scholars Baroque Ensemble — 8.550667–68

[29] **Composer Pronunciation Guide** — 6:35

TOTAL TIME:
69:05

Answers

These are the answers to the numbered
questions asked by the music bird.

1. **a** Lively
2. **b** Jerky
3. It has little gaps where you hear no sound.
4. **a** Quiet
5. It changes: it becomes much slower for about 20 seconds at 1:28.
6. **b** Rhythm
7. **c** Smooth
8. **a** Slow and heavy
9. **b** Plucking the strings

10. **a** Running
11. There are other instruments in the piece too. It is a 'concerto', so it is for an orchestra as well as a flute and harp.
12. **b** Flute
13. **a** Jumpy
14. Yes, the snare drums never stop playing!
15. Yes, it comes back at 0:34.
16. **b** Major key
17. 'born'